D1015785

LE CORDON BLEU

HOME COLLECTION

·CHICKEN·

PERIPLUS
EDITIONS

contents

recipe ratings ✷ *easy* ✷✷ *a little more care needed* ✷✷✷ *more care needed*

Roast chicken

Roast chicken is an all-time favorite with many families—the tantalizing smell, crisp golden skin and snowy-white flesh all add up to a traditional Sunday lunch. Use free-range for a wonderful rich flavor.

*Preparation time **30 minutes***
*Total cooking time **1 hour 40 minutes***
Serves 4

I chicken, about 3 1/2 lb.
1/4 cup oil
1/4 cup unsalted butter
7 oz. chicken wings (about 3)
I shallot, chopped
I tablespoon chopped celery
I tablespoon chopped carrot
I tablespoon chopped onion
bouquet garni (see page 63)

1 Preheat the oven to 400°F. Truss the chicken for roasting by following the method in the Chef's techniques on page 62. Coat the bottom of a roasting pan with a tablespoon of oil. Season the chicken with salt and pepper and rub with the remaining oil. Put the chicken on its side in the roasting pan and place the butter on top. Put in the oven and roast, basting every 5 minutes. After 15 minutes, turn the chicken onto its other side, continuing to baste every 5 minutes. After 15 minutes, turn the chicken onto its back and add the chicken wings. Roast, basting as before, for another 20–30 minutes, or until the juices run clear.

2 Transfer the chicken and wings to an ovenproof plate, cover with foil, set aside and keep warm in a 250°F oven. Place the roasting pan on the stove top over low heat to clarify the fat. After 10 minutes, without stirring, the fat should be clear. Pour off the excess fat. Strain the chicken wings of excess fat and return to the roasting pan. Add the chopped vegetables and cook for 2 minutes, then add 2 cups water and the bouquet garni. Stir to loosen any bits stuck to the roasting pan, then pour into a saucepan. Bring to a boil, reduce the heat and simmer, skimming off the fat occasionally, for about 35 minutes, or until reduced in volume by three quarters. Strain and season with salt and pepper.

3 To serve, remove the string and place the chicken on a platter. Serve the roasting juices in a gravy boat.

Chef's tip To check that a chicken is cooked doesn't require any fancy gadgets or thermometers. Simply lift the chicken by inserting a carving fork into the cavity and allow the juices to drain. If the juices run clear, the chicken is cooked. If the juices have a pink tinge, give the bird another 5–10 minutes in the oven before testing it again.

Chicken liver pâté

Chicken livers have a mild flavor and soft creaminess. Take care not to overcook a pâté—this one should be moist and juicy, with the bacon wrapping adding a contrast of flavor and texture.

*Preparation time **35 minutes + marinating***
  + resting twice overnight
*Total cooking time **1 hour 15 minutes***
Serves 4–6

1¹/₂ tablespoons unsalted butter
I small shallot, finely chopped
6 oz. chicken livers, trimmed and cut in half
10 oz. boneless pork blade, cubed
I teaspoon brandy
I teaspoon port
¹/₈ teaspoon five-spice powder
6 slices bacon
¹/₄ cup heavy cream
I small egg, beaten

1 Heat the butter in a large skillet, add the shallot and heat through for 2 minutes. Remove from the heat, add the livers and pork and stir over very low heat for 3 minutes, or until the meat and liver are warm. Mix in the brandy, port and five-spice, season well with salt and pepper and cover with plastic wrap. Cool slightly, then refrigerate overnight.

2 Preheat the oven to 500°F. Line a 2¹/₂-cup deep terrine or mold with some of the bacon and refrigerate until ready to use. Grind the marinated livers and meat through a meat grinder set with a fine disk or in a food processor. Mix in the cream and egg, spoon into the terrine and cover with the remaining bacon.

3 Bake for 30 minutes, or until the top has begun to brown, then turn the oven to its lowest temperature. Cook for another 30–40 minutes, or until the tip of a small knife, inserted into the center of the pâté for a few seconds, comes out hot. Remove from the oven and allow to cool for 20 minutes. Cut a piece of cardboard or wood to just smaller than the terrine and cover with foil. Place this directly onto the pâté (just inside the edge of the terrine), weigh down with heavy cans and refrigerate for 8 hours or overnight.

4 To unmold, first loosen the edges with a knife and then place the terrine in hot water for 30 seconds. Turn over onto a serving dish and lift away the terrine. Slice the pâté and serve with small gherkins and salad.

Warm chicken and mushroom salad

The warmth of the chicken and mushroom brings out the tangy flavor of the Dijon dressing.

*Preparation time **20 minutes***
*Total cooking time **15 minutes***
Serves 4

2 skinless, boneless chicken breast halves
oil, for cooking
3 tablespoons unsalted butter
7 oz. mixed wild mushrooms, trimmed
1 shallot, finely chopped
5–6 cups mixed salad leaves
2 teaspoons Dijon mustard
2 teaspoons red wine vinegar
1/3 cup olive oil
sprigs of fresh chervil or parsley, to garnish

1 Season the chicken with salt and pepper, then heat a little oil in a skillet and fry for 4 minutes on each side, or until tender. Remove from the pan, cover with foil and set aside.

2 Heat a little more oil in the pan, add the butter and fry the mushrooms for 3–5 minutes, or until tender and lightly colored. Add the shallot and cook for 1 minute. Season to taste and remove with a slotted spoon.

3 Wash and dry the salad leaves and tear into bite-size pieces. Set aside in a large bowl. Remove the foil from the chicken and slice at an angle lengthwise.

4 Whisk together the mustard and vinegar. Continue whisking and slowly add the oil. Pour half the dressing over the salad leaves and toss well; place a mound in the center of each plate. Toss the mushrooms in half the remaining dressing and sprinkle over the salad. Arrange the chicken on top. Drizzle with the remaining dressing and garnish with sprigs of fresh chervil or parsley.

Chicken soup

There are few dishes as comforting as chicken soup—serve with crusty bread for instant inner warmth. This one, with its mirepoix of tiny chopped vegetables, is elegant enough for dinner with guests.

*Preparation time **1 hour***
*Total cooking time **2 hours 15 minutes***
Serves 4–6

1 chicken, about 3¹/₂ lb., trussed (see page 62)
8 large chicken wings, disjointed
1 carrot, quartered lengthwise
1 onion, quartered
1 leek, quartered lengthwise
1 stalk celery, halved
bouquet garni (see page 63)
1 teaspoon salt
¹/₂ cup diced leeks
²/₃ cup diced carrots
²/₃ cup diced turnips
¹/₂ cup diced celery
2 cups diced potatoes
¹/₃ cup peas
¹/₂ cup diced green beans
³/₄ cup diced cabbage
¹/₄ cup unsalted butter

1 Place the chicken and wings in a large stockpot and cover with 6 quarts water. Bring to a boil, reduce the heat and simmer for 10 minutes, skimming off any fat. Add the quartered carrot, onion, leek, halved celery, bouquet garni and salt and simmer for 35 minutes. Remove the chicken and cool. Increase the heat and boil the liquid for 30 minutes. Strain and set the stock aside.

2 Melt the butter in a large stockpot. Add the leek, carrot, turnip and celery and cook slowly for 5 minutes with a pinch of salt, being careful not to allow to color. Add the potato with a pinch of salt and cook gently for 5 minutes. Add 2 quarts of the chicken stock and simmer for 15 minutes, skimming the fat and foam from the surface.

3 Blanch separately the peas, green beans and cabbage in boiling salted water for 5 minutes each. Refresh in iced water, drain and add to the soup. Simmer for another 15 minutes, or until the vegetables are tender.

4 Remove the skin from the cooled chicken and dice the meat. Add to the soup and simmer for 5 minutes. Check the seasoning, season to taste with salt and freshly ground black pepper if necessary, and serve.

Southern-fried chicken

Breaded chicken, fried to crisp perfection—this is one of the classic dishes from the Deep South. A great family favorite for eating with your fingers.

*Preparation time **1 hour + marinating***
*Total cooking time **1 hour***
Serves 4

1 chicken, about 3 1/4 lb.
5 cups buttermilk
2 tablespoons hot red pepper sauce
1 1/3 cups all-purpose flour
1 teaspoon sweet paprika
1 teaspoon dried oregano
1/2 teaspoon cayenne pepper
2 eggs
2 tablespoons oil
3 cups fresh bread crumbs
2 tablespoons unsalted butter
oil, for pan-frying

1 Cut the chicken into eight pieces, following the method in the Chef's techniques on page 63. In a large bowl, combine the buttermilk with the pepper sauce and season to taste with salt. Marinate the chicken for at least 1 hour, or preferably overnight in the refrigerator.

2 Drain the chicken and pat dry. Mix together the flour, paprika, oregano, 1 teaspoon salt and cayenne pepper in a dish and use to coat the chicken. Shake off the excess and set the chicken aside.

3 Beat the eggs with the oil and 2 tablespoons water. Dip the chicken pieces into the egg mixture, then roll in the bread crumbs and press well. Place on a plate lined with paper towels. Preheat the oven to 300°F.

4 Heat the butter with about 1 inch oil in a large heavy-bottomed skillet over medium-high heat. Add the chicken, skin-side-down, and reduce the heat to medium. Cook for about 10 minutes, or until nicely browned. If necessary, cook in batches—do not crowd the pan, and leave enough space between the pieces to ensure even cooking. Turn the pieces over and cook until browned. Transfer to a baking dish or roasting pan, cover loosely with foil and bake for 45 minutes. Drain on paper towels and serve immediately.

Chef's tips If you want to make a spicier dish, simply add a tablespoon of curry paste to the marinade.

Curry paste is available from good supermarkets and specialty stores.

Chicken chasseur

This classic French pan-fried chicken with a mushroom sauce is easy to prepare and will fully satisfy any guest. The recipe may be traditional but it's also versatile—try adding onions, wild mushrooms, tomatoes or bacon to the sauce. Delicious with crusty bread or roast potatoes.

*Preparation time **30 minutes***
*Total cooking time **1 hour 30 minutes***
Serves 4

1 chicken, about 2¹/₂ lb., giblets optional
1¹/₂ cups chicken stock (see page 62)
oil, for cooking
1²/₃ cups sliced button mushrooms
1 large shallot, finely chopped
2 tablespoons brandy
2 tablespoons white wine
2–3 large sprigs fresh tarragon
2–3 sprigs fresh chervil

1 Preheat the oven to 400°F. Cut the chicken into four or eight pieces, following the method in the Chef's techniques on page 63, then coarsely cut up the remaining carcass with a knife or poultry shears.
2 Put the carcass pieces and giblets, if using, into a roasting pan and roast for 25 minutes, or until browned. Remove from the oven and add the stock. Use a wooden spoon to loosen any bits stuck to the pan and simmer gently on the stove top for 30 minutes. Strain and reserve the liquid. Skim off any excess fat.
3 On the stove top, heat a little oil in the clean roasting pan, add the chicken pieces, skin-side-down, and brown quickly and lightly on both sides. Transfer to the oven to finish cooking: the legs will need 20 minutes, the breast and wings 15 minutes. Check that the chicken is cooked by piercing with a fork or fine skewer—the juices should run clear. Remove from the pan and keep warm.
4 Pour the excess fat from the pan, leaving 1 tablespoon and any chicken juices. Reheat on top of the stove, then add the mushrooms and cook until lightly browned. Add the shallot and cook without browning. Increase the heat if necessary and, when the pan is very hot, add the brandy. Bring to a boil and light with a match to flambé. Add the white wine and reduce the heat to simmer for 1–2 minutes, or until reduced by half. Add the reserved chicken stock and reduce for 4–5 minutes. Season to taste with salt and pepper. Finely chop the herbs and add to the sauce—do not allow to boil again. Spoon over the chicken to serve.

Deep-fried chicken with cumin and sesame

Sesame seeds for crisp crunchy batter and a tangy dipping sauce for an eastern twist.

Preparation time **20 minutes**
Total cooking time **20 minutes**
Serves **4**

2/3 cup all-purpose flour
1/2 cup potato starch
1 teaspoon baking powder
2 teaspoons oil
1/2 cup sesame seeds
1/4 teaspoon ground cumin
3 small skinless, boneless chicken breast halves
oil, for deep-frying

DIPPING SAUCE
1/2 teaspoon grated fresh ginger root
1 teaspoon finely chopped scallion
1 tablespoon vinegar
1 tablespoon soy sauce
2 tablespoons ketchup
1 teaspoon sesame oil

1 Sift together the flour, potato starch, baking powder and a good pinch of salt into a bowl. Add the oil and whisk while adding 2/3 cup water in a steady stream. Whisk until the batter is smooth, add the sesame seeds and cumin and cover with plastic wrap.

2 To make the dipping sauce, mix together all the ingredients and set aside.

3 Trim the chicken of excess fat and cut lengthwise into thin strips. Season with salt and pepper, dip in the batter and deep-fry in moderately hot oil at 375°F until golden. Drain on paper towels and serve immediately with the dipping sauce served alongside.

Cider apple chicken with mushroom sauce

The traditional French name for this recipe is Poulet Vallée d'Auge. *The Auge Valley
is in Normandy and this recipe makes good use of local ingredients: butter, Calvados, cider,
cream and apples from the dairy farms and apple orchards.*

Preparation time **25 minutes**
Total cooking time **1 hour**
Serves 4

1 chicken (about 3¹/2 lb.)
1/4 cup unsalted butter
oil, for cooking
1/4 cup Calvados or applejack
2 shallots, finely chopped
2 cups hard cider
1²/3 cups sliced button mushrooms
1 cup heavy cream
1–2 Golden Delicious apples
3 tablespoons clarified butter (see Chef's tip)
1/4 cup chopped fresh parsley

1 Cut the chicken into four or eight pieces, following the method in the Chef's techniques on page 63, and season with salt and pepper. Heat half the butter and a little oil in a skillet and sauté the chicken in batches, skin-side-down, until lightly browned. Pour off the excess fat, return all the chicken to the pan, add the Calvados or applejack and light with a match to flambé (keep a saucepan lid on one side in case of emergency).

Add the shallots and cook gently until softened but not brown. Add the cider, cover and cook for 15 minutes, turning the chicken after 10 minutes.

2 Meanwhile, sauté the mushrooms in the remaining butter, covered, for 4 minutes. Add the mushrooms and cooking juices, and the cream to the chicken and cook for 5 minutes. Remove the chicken and keep warm.

3 Continue cooking the sauce for 10 minutes, or until it is reduced enough to coat the back of a spoon. Adjust the seasoning to taste. Return the chicken to the pan, bring to a boil, reduce the heat and simmer for 2 minutes to heat the chicken through.

4 Core the unpeeled apples and cut across into thin slices. Fry in clarified butter until golden brown on both sides. Garnish the chicken with the apples and parsley.

Chef's tip Clarified butter is used because it will cook at a higher temperature without burning. You will need about 1/3 cup butter to yield about 3 tablespoons clarified butter. Melt the butter gently over low heat in a small heavy-bottomed pan, without stirring or shaking the pan. Skim the froth from the top, then carefully pour the clear butter into another container, leaving the white sediment in the base of the pan. Cover and keep in the refrigerator for up to 4 weeks.

Chicken en croûte

Succulent chicken breasts, married with mushrooms and bacon and encased in crisp braided pastry. This dish requires a little patience in the making, but the results are spectacular.

*Preparation time **1 hour + 40 minutes chilling***
*Total cooking time **1 hour 30 minutes***
Serves 4

oil, for cooking
4 skinless, boneless chicken breast halves
2 tablespoons unsalted butter
I shallot, finely chopped
I clove garlic, finely chopped
2³/4 cups finely chopped mushrooms
2 sheets frozen pre-rolled puff pastry, thawed
4 thin slices slab bacon or pancetta, rind removed
I egg, lightly beaten

SAUCE
¹/4 cup oil
4 chicken wings, disjointed
I onion, finely chopped
2 carrots, finely chopped
I stalk celery, finely chopped
I mushroom, finely chopped
I bay leaf
I tablespoon sherry vinegar
¹/3 cup dry Madeira or sherry
2 cups chicken stock (see page 62)

1 Heat about ¹/4 cup oil in a skillet and fry the chicken for 1 minute on each side to seal. Remove from the pan and set aside.

2 Heat the butter in a medium-sized saucepan, add the shallot and garlic, cover with waxed paper and a lid and cook very gently until transparent and soft. Add the mushrooms and increase the heat. The mushrooms will produce juice, so cook uncovered until dry. Season with salt and pepper, then transfer to a plate to cool.

3 Roll out each sheet of pastry on a lightly floured surface to a 12 x 10-inch rectangle, then cut in half to make two 10 x 6-inch rectanlges. Transfer to two lightly floured baking sheets and chill for 20 minutes. Slide each off the sheet onto a lightly floured work surface and make cuts at about 3/4-inch intervals down the two short sides of each rectangle. Make the cuts 3 inches long, towards the center of the rectangle.

4 Place a chicken breast down the center of each pastry rectangle. Put a quarter of the mushroom mixture on each chicken breast and lightly flatten, then cover with bacon or pancetta, folding around to hold the mushroom in place. Brush the pastry strips with egg. Take the top strip of pastry from one side and place over the chicken. Take the top strip from the other side and place on top, as if to braid. Continue down the chicken, overlapping slightly and leaving small gaps between the braiding to let the steam escape and the pastry crispen. Trim the strips at the base of the chicken or tuck underneath. Place on a buttered baking sheet and chill for 20 minutes. Preheat the oven to 400°F.

5 To make the sauce, add the oil to a roasting pan and heat on top of the stove. Add the wings then roast for 30 minutes, or until golden brown. Transfer to the stove top, add the chopped vegetables, bay leaf and vinegar and simmer for 5 minutes, or until reduced by three quarters and the pan juices are sticky. Add the Madeira or sherry and bring to a boil, add the stock, reduce the heat and simmer gently for 10 minutes, or until reduced by half. Skim frequently with a spoon. Strain into a clean saucepan and season to taste.

6 Brush the pastry parcels with egg, avoiding the cut edges or they will not rise. Bake for 25–30 minutes, or until golden and crisp. If the underside is not crisp, cover the top with foil and cook a little longer. Serve with the sauce and steamed asparagus spears.

Breast of chicken with tarragon and mustard sauce

The perennial aromatic herb French tarragon has a subtle anise-like flavor, which perfectly complements other gently flavored foods such as eggs, fish and chicken. The Latin name means "little dragon," from the belief that the herb could cure the bites of venomous creatures.

Preparation time **15 minutes**
Total cooking time **50 minutes**
Serves 4

oil, for cooking
4 skinless, boneless chicken breast halves
4 shallots, thinly sliced
1/3 cup dry white wine
2 cups chicken stock (see page 62)
3/4 cup heavy cream or crème fraîche
2–3 tablespoons Dijon or tarragon mustard, to taste
2–3 tablespoons fresh tarragon leaves

1 Preheat the oven to 350°F. Heat about 1 tablespoon oil in a roasting pan on the stove top and fry the chicken breasts for 5 minutes on each side, or until golden brown. Transfer to the oven and cook for another 5–10 minutes, or until the juices run clear when a skewer is inserted into the center.

2 Remove the chicken from the pan and keep warm. Spoon off the excess fat and transfer the roasting pan to the stove top. Add the shallots and fry until soft and lightly browned, then add the wine and reduce until almost dry. Add the stock and simmer for 5–10 minutes, or until syrupy.

3 Strain the sauce into a clean saucepan, add the cream and simmer for 5 minutes. Stir in the mustard and season with salt and pepper to taste. Chop the tarragon and sprinkle into the sauce at the last minute to prevent it discoloring. Serve the sauce over the chicken.

Chef's tip The shallots, which have a lovely flavor, could be left in the sauce. If you wish to do this, simply add the cream without straining the sauce first.

Coronation chicken

Originally created by Rosemary Hume of The Cordon Bleu Cookery School, London, for the foreign dignitaries at the coronation luncheon of Queen Elizabeth II, this dish now appears on menus around the world. Here is an updated version of the traditional recipe.

*Preparation time **30 minutes + cooling***
*Total cooking time **1 hour***
Serves 4

I chicken, about 3 lb.
I carrot, sliced
I onion, halved
bouquet garni (see page 63)
6 peppercorns
oil, for cooking
2 shallots, finely chopped
I teaspoon curry powder
2 teaspoons tomato paste
1/4 cup red wine
pinch of sugar
I slice lemon
few drops of lemon juice
I tablespoon mango chutney
I cup mayonnaise
1/4–1/3 cup lightly whipped cream
chopped scallion, to garnish

1 Place the chicken, carrot, onion, bouquet garni, peppercorns and a pinch of salt in a large saucepan, add enough water to cover and bring to a boil. Reduce the heat and simmer for about 40 minutes, or until tender. Leave the chicken to cool in the liquid. When cold, remove the chicken and discard the skin and bones. Cut the chicken meat into bite-size pieces and set aside.

2 Heat a little oil in a large saucepan, add the shallots and cook gently for 3–4 minutes. Add the curry powder and continue to cook for 1–2 minutes. Add the tomato paste, wine and 2 tablespoons water and bring to a boil. Add the sugar, salt and pepper to taste, and the lemon and lemon juice. Reduce the heat and simmer for 5–10 minutes, or until reduced by half. Stir in the mango chutney, strain and cool.

3 Once the mixture has cooled, gradually add to the mayonnaise, to taste. Adjust the seasoning, adding a little more lemon juice if necessary. Stir in the whipped cream and chicken. Garnish with a little scallion. Delicious served with rice salad.

Chef's tip For a rice salad that is perfect to serve with Coronation chicken, mix together 1 cup cooked rice with cubes of cooked carrot, strips of red sweet bell pepper, sliced celery, cooked peas and peeled, seeded and quartered tomatoes. Whisk together oil and vinegar and toss over the salad to moisten.

Braised chicken and cilantro roulade with turmeric and almonds

This clever technique is so simple—the chicken breast is cut open then rolled around the fresh cilantro. After cooking, the roll is sliced to reveal a colorful, moist filling.

*Preparation time **30 minutes***
*Total cooking time **15 minutes***
Serves 4

4 skinless, boneless chicken breast halves,
  about 5 oz. each
I cup fresh cilantro leaves
oil, for cooking
4 teaspoons ground turmeric
2 cups chicken stock
  (see page 62)
2/3 cup whole blanched almonds

1 Preheat the oven to 400°F. Lay the chicken breasts flat on a cutting board, putting a hand flat on top to gently hold the meat in place. Slice into the side of each breast until you have cut two thirds across, then open the breast like a book. Place a layer of cilantro on top of each breast, reserving some to garnish, and season with salt and pepper. Roll up the breasts from the bottom to enclose the cilantro and secure the rolls with string.

2 Heat 2–3 tablespoons oil in a heavy-bottomed flameproof casserole or Dutch oven over high heat. When very hot, add the chicken rolls and brown quickly on all sides. Remove the chicken from the pan, pour off the oil and add the turmeric. Return the chicken rolls to the pan and shake until they are well coated with turmeric. Add the stock and bring to a boil. Add the almonds, cover and place the casserole in the oven for 8–10 minutes, or until the rolls have cooked through.

3 Remove the rolls from the liquid, cover to prevent drying out and leave in a warm place. Strain the cooking liquid. Place the almonds in a blender or food processor, add 1/3 cup of the cooking liquid and purée until smooth. Gradually add more of the liquid and process until the sauce has a flowing consistency. Season to taste with salt and pepper.

4 Remove the string and cut across the chicken rolls into six slices each. Arrange the slices on a hot plate and pour some sauce around. Garnish with the cilantro leaves to serve.

Deviled Poussin

Poussin is the French name for baby chicken. You can use either baby chickens (squab) or small Cornish hens for this treatment with equally moist and tender results.

Preparation time **30 minutes**
Total cooking time **1 hour**
Serves 4

4 baby chickens or Cornish hens, about 14 oz. each
melted butter or oil, for cooking
1/4 cup Dijon or mild English mustard
3/4 cup fresh bread crumbs
chopped fresh parsley, to garnish

1 Remove the wishbones from the chickens, following the method in the Chef's techniques on page 63, and preheat the oven to 350°F.

2 To open and flatten the chickens, rinse out the inside cavity, then with the breast-side-down, use poultry shears to cut along each side of the backbone and remove it. Turn the chickens breast-side-up and push down with the weight of two flat hands to break the breastbone. Tuck the wing tips under the breast. Run a skewer between the two bones of one of the middle wing joints, then through the breast and out through to the wing on the other side. Push another metal skewer through from one thigh to the other. Lay the chickens flat, breast-side-up, on an oiled broiler pan.

3 Brush with the butter or oil and season lightly with salt and pepper. Place under a slow broiler to lightly color, then roast in the oven for 40–50 minutes, or until the juices run clear.

4 Spread the chicken skin evenly with the mustard, sprinkle with bread crumbs, then drizzle with a little melted butter or oil. Place under a hot broiler until golden brown and garnish with parsley to serve.

Coq au vin

The long list of ingredients is not as daunting as it appears. The chicken is marinated overnight in wine, vegetables and herbs to tenderize and flavor it, and the dish can quickly be put together the next day. This traditional recipe originated in the Burgundy region, famous for its fine red wines.

*Preparation time **50 minutes + overnight marinating***
*Total cooking time **2 hours***
*Serves **6–8***

MARINADE
1 onion, chopped
1 carrot, chopped
5 juniper berries
10 peppercorns
1 whole clove
1 clove garlic
2 quarts red wine
1/4 cup Cognac or brandy
2 tablespoons red wine vinegar
bouquet garni (see page 63)

6 lb. chicken pieces
clarified butter or oil, for cooking
1/3 cup all-purpose flour
3 cups chicken stock (see page 62)
6 oz. slab bacon
3 small boiling onions
4 teaspoons sugar
1 tablespoon unsalted butter
15 button mushrooms

CROUTONS
4 slices bread, crusts removed
2/3 cup clarified butter or oil
1 tablespoon chopped fresh parsley

1 To make the marinade, place all the ingredients into a large nonreactive bowl. Add the chicken pieces, cover and leave overnight in the refrigerator.

2 Remove the chicken pieces and dry with paper towels. Strain the marinade and reserve the vegetables and herbs separately from the liquid. Preheat the oven to 400°F.

3 Heat a little clarified butter or oil in a deep flameproof casserole or Dutch oven and sauté the chicken over high heat, skin-side-down first, until well browned on all sides. Add the reserved marinated vegetables and herbs. Cook for 5 minutes, or until softened, stirring occasionally. Pour off any excess fat. Sprinkle the flour into the dish and mix well. Add the reserved marinade, hot stock and salt and pepper. Cover with waxed paper and a lid and bake in the oven for 45 minutes, or until the chicken is cooked through. Reduce the oven temperature to 300°F. Remove the chicken to a clean casserole, strain the sauce and skim off the excess fat. Season if necessary. Pour over the chicken and return to the oven to heat through.

4 Meanwhile, put the bacon in a saucepan, cover with water and bring to a boil. Drain, rinse under cold water and trim away the rind. Cut into small pieces and fry in a little oil until golden; drain on paper towels. Put the onions, sugar and butter in a pan with just enough water to cover. Bring to a boil, then simmer until all the water has evaporated and the onions are tender (if necessary, add a little extra water and continue cooking). Glaze the onions by tossing them in the butter and sugar in the pan until golden. Fry the mushrooms in hot oil and drain. Sprinkle the bacon, onions and mushrooms over the chicken, cover and keep warm.

5 To make croutons, cut each slice of bread into four triangles and pan-fry in very hot clarified butter or oil until golden brown—be careful as the bread browns quickly. Dip the tips of the croutons in the parsley and arrange over the dish.

Stuffed chicken breast with cucumber

The cucumber's origins date back to Roman times and with its cool and refreshing qualities it is included in many of today's recipes. This dish is beautifully light and brings a taste of summer all year-round.

Preparation time **35 minutes + 20 minutes chilling**
Total cooking time **40 minutes**
Serves 6

I chicken leg and thigh quarter, skinned
I egg white
2¼ cups heavy cream
I cup chopped mixed fresh herbs
6 skinless, boneless chicken breast halves,
about 6 oz. each
I large cucumber, not waxed
3 shallots, finely chopped
⅓ cup dry white wine
2 cups chicken stock (see page 62)

1 Cut the chicken flesh from the bones of the leg and thigh, and purée in a food processor. Lightly beat the egg white and add just over half of it to the chicken (discard the remainder). Season with salt and pepper, then use the pulse button to mix in 3/4 cup cream and the herbs. Do not overprocess or the cream may separate. Cover and chill for 15–20 minutes to firm up slightly.

2 Remove the thin tenderloin strips from the underside of the chicken breasts and place on lightly oiled plastic wrap or waxed paper. Gently flatten them with a meat mallet or small heavy-bottomed pan and store in the refrigerator.

3 Make a short slit on the top of each chicken breast and make a pocket by cutting just under either side of the slit with the tip of a sharp knife. Using a spoon or pastry bag, fill each pocket with the chicken purée; do not overfill or it will burst in cooking. Place a flattened chicken strip over the top of each breast to completely cover the chicken purée. Wrap each breast in buttered foil, twisting the ends tightly to seal. Poach in gently simmering water for 20–30 minutes. Remove from the heat and leave to rest in the hot poaching liquid.

4 Cut the unpeeled cucumber in half lengthwise and, using the point of a teaspoon, scrape out the seeds. Cut three-quarters of the cucumber into 2-inch lengths and cut into strips about the thickness of a little finger. Blanch in a small pan of boiling salted water for 2–3 minutes, rinse under cold water and drain. Coarsely chop the remaining cucumber and set aside.

5 To make the sauce, place the shallots, wine and chicken stock in a wide saucepan and quickly bring to a boil. Boil the sauce for 5 minutes, or until it has reduced to a light syrupy consistency. Add the remaining 1½ cups cream and boil until the mixture thickens slightly. Add the chopped cucumber and boil for another 5 minutes. Transfer the sauce to a blender or food processor and purée well. Season with salt and pepper and strain through a sieve.

6 Serve the chicken breasts immediately, either whole or sliced, with the cucumber strips and sauce.

Chicken Basque

The Basque country is located in the south-west of France and northern Spain, close to the Pyrenees mountains. This traditional recipe uses local produce such as onions, sweet peppers, tomatoes and garlic but we have substituted the more readily available Parma ham or prosciutto for the local cured ham from Bayonne, and olive oil instead of the traditional goose fat.

Preparation time 30 minutes
Total cooking time 1 hour 15 minutes
Serves 4

2 red sweet bell peppers
2 green sweet bell peppers
2 medium tomatoes
1 chicken, about 2 lb 6 oz
oil, for cooking
1 large onion, thinly sliced
3 cloves garlic, crushed
1/3 cup white wine
3 oz. Parma ham or prosciutto, cut into strips
1 tablespoon chopped fresh parsley, to garnish

1 Halve the peppers, remove the seeds and membrane and slice the flesh into long strips. Score a cross in the base of each tomato, then plunge into boiling water for 10 seconds. Rinse with cold water and peel the skin away from the cross. Quarter and remove the seeds.

2 Cut the chicken into eight pieces, following the method in the Chef's techniques on page 63. Season with salt and pepper. Heat about 2 tablespoons oil in a large deep skillet. Add the chicken pieces, skin-side-down first, and fry until light golden brown all over. Remove and drain on crumpled paper towels.

3 Spoon off the excess oil, leaving just 1 tablespoon in the pan. Add the onion, garlic, peppers and tomatoes and simmer for 10 minutes. Add the white wine, cover and simmer for another 30 minutes. Add the chicken, season lightly with salt and pepper, cover and simmer for 15–20 minutes. Check that the chicken is fully cooked by piercing it with a fork (the juices should run clear). Lift out the chicken pieces, cover with foil and keep warm. Season the sauce with salt and pepper to taste.

4 Pan-fry the ham or prosciutto in a little oil, lifting directly from the pan with a slotted spoon, without draining on paper towels. Pour the sauce over the chicken, sprinkle with the ham or prosciutto and garnish with the parsley.

Chicken fricassee with spring vegetables

The word fricassee is French in origin and may have been a marriage of two culinary terms: frire, *which means to fry, and* casse, *meaning ladle or dripping pan.*

Preparation time **25 minutes**
Total cooking time **1 hour**
Serves 4

1 chicken, about 3¹/2 lb.
¹/4 cup all-purpose flour, seasoned with salt and
    pepper
oil, for cooking
2 tablespoons unsalted butter
6 shallots, thinly sliced
¹/3 cup dry white wine
1 cup chicken stock (see page 62)
bouquet garni (see page 63)
1 egg yolk
²/3 cup sour cream
8 baby carrots
8 baby turnips
4 small boiling onions
1 teaspoon sugar
2 cups trimmed snow peas
12 asparagus spears
9 button mushrooms

1 Cut the chicken into eight pieces, following the method in the Chef's techniques on page 63. Coat the chicken pieces in the seasoned flour, shaking off and reserving the excess. Heat a little oil in a large skillet over medium heat, add 1 tablespoon of the butter and cook the chicken quickly to seal without coloring; remove from the pan and set aside. Lower the heat, add the shallots to the pan and cook slowly, without coloring, until softened. Stir in the reserved flour, then pour in the wine, stirring until the mixture boils and thickens. Reduce the heat and simmer for 2 minutes, then stir in the stock and bouquet garni. Return the chicken to the pan, cover and simmer for 15 minutes. Remove the wings and breast meat, keeping them covered and warm, and cook for another 5 minutes. Remove the chicken thighs and legs, leaving the cooking liquid in the pan.

2 Increase the heat and let the liquid boil for 5–10 minutes, or until reduced by half, skimming off the excess fat with a spoon. Mix the egg yolk with a tablespoon of sour cream in a bowl. Stir the remaining sour cream into the pan and bring to a boil, then simmer for 2 minutes. Remove from the heat, pour a little hot sauce onto the egg yolk mixture, blend and return to the pan, whisking or stirring until heated (do not allow to boil). Strain, season to taste and set aside.

3 Place the carrots, turnips and boiling onions in separate small pans with just enough water to cover. Add a small pinch of salt, sugar and a third of the remaining butter to each pan, then press on buttered waxed paper to cover. Cook gently until the water has nearly evaporated and the vegetables are cooked and shiny, shaking the pan occasionally. Remove to a lightly buttered dish, arrange in separate piles and keep warm.

4 Cook the snow peas, asparagus and mushrooms in salted boiling water for 3–5 minutes, or until tender but still crisp. Drain well.

5 Lay a piece of chicken breast and dark meat on each serving plate and coat with the sauce. Serve with the vegetables alongside.

Tarragon and tomato chicken

*This recipe comes from Lyon, France's third largest city and its gastronomic capital,
situated close to the Burgundy vineyards.*

Preparation time **20 minutes**
Total cooking time **45 minutes**
Serves 4

1 chicken, about 2¹/₂ lb.
oil or butter, for cooking
3/4 cup tarragon vinegar (see Chef's tip)
2 lb. tomatoes
1 tablespoon unsalted butter, softened
2 tablespoons all-purpose flour
sprig of fresh tarragon, to garnish

1 Cut the chicken into four or eight pieces, following the method in the Chef's techniques on page 63, and season with salt and pepper. Heat a little oil or butter in a skillet and brown the chicken on all sides, skin-side-down first. Do not crowd the pan so, if necessary, brown the chicken in batches. Remove the chicken and pour off any excess oil from the pan.

2 Return all the chicken to the pan and add half of the tarragon vinegar. Cover and simmer for 10 minutes.

Turn the chicken pieces over, cover and cook for another 10 minutes, or until the juices run clear when pierced with a fork. Remove the chicken from the pan. Cover the pan and keep the sauce warm.

3 Score a cross in the base of each tomato, then plunge into boiling water for 10 seconds. Rinse with cold water and peel the skin away from the cross. Cut in half, remove the seeds, then cut into eighths. Put the remaining vinegar in a saucepan and boil for 4 minutes. Mix together the softened butter and flour, whisk into the reduced vinegar and then whisk this into the sauce. Return the chicken to the sauce, add the tomatoes and simmer for 10 minutes, or until the sauce just coats the back of a spoon. Check the seasoning. Chop the fresh tarragon just before serving, sprinkle over the chicken and serve with rice.

Chef's tip Make your own tarragon vinegar by placing a sprig of fresh tarragon into a bottle of ordinary red or white wine vinegar. After a week, strain out the tarragon and your vinegar is ready. All your favorite herbs can be used in this way.

Chicken Kiev

You can pan-fry or deep-fry your Chicken Kiev to produce a crisp coating for the chicken and garlic butter, which bursts with succulence and flavor as you cut into it.

Preparation time **40 minutes**
Total cooking time **40 minutes**
Serves 4

4 skinless, boneless chicken breast halves
I cup all-purpose flour, seasoned with salt and pepper
3 eggs, beaten
2¹/2 cups fine dry bread crumbs
oil, for cooking and deep-frying

GARLIC BUTTER
²/3 cup unsalted butter
3 cloves garlic, minced
³/4 cup chopped fresh parsley

1 Remove the thin tenderloin strips from the underside of the chicken breasts and place them on lightly oiled plastic wrap or greaseproof or waxed paper. Gently flatten them with a meat mallet or small heavy-bottomed pan and put in the refrigerator.

2 To make the garlic butter, soften the butter, then add the garlic, parsley, salt and pepper, and mix well. Spoon the butter along one end of a piece of oiled plastic wrap or damp greaseproof or waxed paper and roll it up into a sausage shape, twisting the ends. Refrigerate until firm.

3 Cut a short slit into the top of each chicken breast and make a pocket by cutting just under either side of the slit with the tip of a small sharp knife. Carefully place a slice of the firm garlic butter into each pocket. Place a flattened chicken strip over the top of each chicken breast to completely cover the butter.

4 Place the seasoned flour, egg and bread crumbs in separate shallow dishes. Coat the chicken with the flour, then with the egg and finally with the bread crumbs. Coat again with the egg and bread crumbs.

5 Preheat the oven to 400°F. To pan-fry, heat enough oil in a skillet to come halfway up the sides of the chicken. Cook the Kievs over medium heat for 6 minutes each side, or until golden brown and cooked through. Transfer to a wire rack in the oven for a few minutes to allow the coating to crispen.

6 To deep-fry, preheat the oil in a deep saucepan to 325°F. Add two of the chicken breasts and fry for 8–12 minutes, or until golden brown. Remove from the oil and drain on crumpled paper towels. Keep warm in the oven on a wire rack while cooking the rest. Serve Chicken Kievs with a crisp salad and fresh bread.

Chicken jalfrezi

*This spicy curry can be found under
many guises—jalfreji, jalfresi and even jhal fry.*

Preparation time **20 minutes**
Total cooking time **55 minutes**
Serves 4

oil, for cooking
I onion, finely grated
2 cloves garlic, chopped
I¹/₂ lb. skinless, boneless chicken thighs, cut in half
I tablespoon ground turmeric
I teaspoon ground red chile powder
I¹/₂ teaspoons salt
16 oz. can crushed tomatoes
2 tablespoons ghee (clarified butter)
I tablespoon ground cumin
I tablespoon ground coriander
2¹/₂ tablespoons grated fresh ginger root
I cup coarsely chopped fresh cilantro leaves

1　Heat about 2 tablespoons oil in a deep skillet and fry
the onion and garlic for 2 minutes over high heat.
2　Add the chicken, turmeric, chile powder and salt. Fry
gently for 5–10 minutes, or until golden brown, scraping
the base of the pan frequently and turning the chicken.
Add the tomatoes, cover and cook over medium heat
for 20 minutes. Uncover and simmer for 10 minutes to
let all the excess liquid evaporate and the sauce thicken.
3　Add the ghee or oil, cumin, ground coriander, ginger
root and fresh cilantro and simmer for 5–7 minutes, or
until the fat separates out from the thick sauce. Season
if necessary. Serve the chicken pieces with the sauce
spooned on top. This dish could be served with basmati
rice, chapatis or naan bread.

Chicken consommé

A consommé is a classic clear soup made from meat, chicken or fish stock.
The name comes from the French word consommer, *meaning to finish up or use up*
and is so called because all the goodness of the meat goes into the soup.

Preparation time **45 minutes**

Total cooking time **3 hours 15 minutes**

Serves 4

2¹/₂ lb. chicken drumsticks

8 oz. lean ground beef

I teaspoon oil

I small carrot, coarsely chopped

I small leek, coarsely chopped

I small stalk celery, coarsely chopped

I small onion, halved

2 whole cloves, stuck into the onion

bouquet garni (see page 63)

I teaspoon salt

6 peppercorns

2 egg whites

TO SERVE

I tablespoon unsalted butter

¹/₂ small leek, white part only,
   cut into julienne strips (see Chef's tips)

¹/₂ small carrot, cut into julienne strips

¹/₂ stalk celery, cut into julienne strips

1 Preheat the oven to 400°F. Remove the skin from the drumsticks and discard. Scrape the meat from the bones, following the method in the Chef's techniques on page 63, place in a food processor and process until finely ground. Place the ground chicken and the beef in a bowl in the refrigerator. Coarsely chop the bones, place in a roasting pan and bake for 30–40 minutes, or until well browned.

2 Heat the oil in a large stockpot, add the carrot, leek and celery and cook until lightly colored. Set aside. Heat a cast-iron or stainless steel skillet and add the onion, cut-side-down. Cook over medium heat until the onion has blackened.

3 Place the bones, carrot, leek, celery, onion, bouquet garni, salt and peppercorns in a large stockpot and cover with 2 quarts cold water. Add the egg whites to the ground meat and mix with a wooden spoon, then add 2 cups water and mix well. Add to the stockpot and mix well. Place the stockpot over medium heat and bring slowly to a boil, stirring every 2 minutes. Reduce the heat and leave to gently simmer for 2 hours. Line a fine sieve with cheesecloth and place over a clean saucepan. Gently ladle the consommé into the sieve and strain into the pan.

4 To serve, melt the butter in a small skillet. Add the julienned vegetables along with a pinch of salt and cook, covered, over low heat for 10–15 minutes, or until the vegetables are cooked but still firm. Strain and pat dry to remove the excess butter, then place in four soup bowls and pour in the hot consommé.

Chef's tips Julienne strips are even-size strips of vegetables which are the size and shape of matchsticks. They cook quickly, are simple to prepare and make attractive decorations for any dish. The strips may be cut into whatever length is desired.

In order to remove the maximum amount of fat, the consommé is best made a day in advance and kept refrigerated overnight, or until the excess fat solidifies on the surface. Simply skim off the fat before reheating the consommé over a pan of gently simmering water.

Lime-marinated chicken with Mediterranean bread

*This refreshing dish combines the flavors of the Mediterranean and the tropics. Lime, yogurt
and cilantro blend especially well together and are complemented by a light, crusty bread.*

Preparation time **50 minutes + rising + marinating**
Total cooking time **55 minutes**
Serves 4

MEDITERRANEAN BREAD (see Chef's tips)
1³/4 cups lukewarm water
1 oz. fresh yeast
5¹/2 cups bread flour or all-purpose flour
¹/2 cup extra virgin olive oil
1 tablespoon salt
²/3 cup pitted black olives, coarsely chopped
²/3 cup sun-dried tomatoes, soaked, drained and
   coarsely chopped (see Chef's tips)

3 cups plain yogurt
2 fresh green chiles, seeded and chopped
2 cloves garlic, chopped
¹/4 cup coarsely chopped fresh cilantro
grated rind of 3 limes
juice of ¹/2 lime
8 skinless, boneless chicken thighs

1 To make the Mediterranean bread, combine the
warm water and yeast in a small bowl and stir together
until smoothly blended. Sift 3¹/2 cups of the flour into
a bowl and make a well in the center. Pour the yeast and
water into the well, followed by the olive oil. Using your
hand with fingers slightly apart, gradually begin to draw
the flour into the liquid in the well. Continue until all
the flour has been incorporated and a loose batter is
formed. Beat for 5 minutes in a slapping motion to
develop its elasticity and free it from lumps. Clean the
sides of the bowl with a scraper, cover with a damp cloth
and leave at room temperature to rise for 1–1¹/2 hours,
or until doubled in volume. Add the remaining flour,
salt, olives and sun-dried tomatoes and mix well. Scrape
down the side of the bowl, cover with a fresh damp
cloth and leave until doubled in volume.

2 Preheat the oven to 400°F. Lightly butter and flour
two medium-size baking sheets. Divide the very soft
dough in half (do not be alarmed by the very loose
texture—this is quite normal). Be careful not to
overhandle the dough or it will lose volume. Place on
the sheets and, with wet hands, gently pat and shape
each piece to a rectangle about 1 inch thick. Sprinkle
with cold water and dust heavily with extra flour. Bake
in the oven for 35–40 minutes, or until a skewer
inserted into the center of the bread comes out clean.
Transfer to a cooling rack and leave for 20 minutes
before serving.

3 For the marinated chicken, combine the yogurt,
chiles, garlic, cilantro and lime rind and juice in a
blender until smooth. Season with salt and pepper. Place
half the mixture in a dish and lay the chicken on top.
Cover with the remaining mixture and leave in a cool
place for 30 minutes. Arrange the chicken on a broiler
tray. Broil slowly, turning frequently, for up to
15 minutes, or until cooked through. Serve with the
Mediterranean bread in slices alongside.

Chef's tips The Mediterranean bread is a perfect
complement to the marinated chicken, but be sure to
prepare it well in advance to allow time for the dough
to rise. The nature of this rustic bread is for it to have an
uneven, crusty texture. The olive oil gives the bread its
unique crustiness and not punching down the dough
during rising creates the holes in the loaf.

If you are using sun-dried tomatoes in oil, there is no
need to soak them before draining and chopping.

Roasted baby chickens with herb butter

This is a deliciously simple variation on a plain roast chicken. Use whichever fresh herbs
you have to hand and pick up the same flavors in the buttery sauce.

Preparation time **40 minutes**
Total cooking time **1 hour 15 minutes**
Serves 4

2 baby chickens (squab) or small Cornish hens,
   about 14 oz. each
¹/3 cup unsalted butter, softened
¹/4 cup chopped mixed fresh herbs
   (tarragon, chervil, parsley)
2 tablespoons oil
3–4 chicken wings, disjointed
2¹/2 tablespoons chopped carrot
2¹/2 tablespoons chopped shallot
2¹/2 tablespoons chopped onion
1 tablespoon chopped celery

1 Preheat the oven to 400°F. Prepare the chickens by gently sliding a finger under the skin at the neck end and loosening the skin from the flesh. Be careful not to tear the skin.

2 In a small bowl, mix together the butter and herbs and season to taste. Using a pastry bag with a small nozzle, pipe about 2 tablespoons herb butter under the skin of each chicken, using your fingers to spread out the butter as much as possible. If you do not have a pastry bag, you can simply use the handle of a fork or spoon to spread the herb butter under the skin. Truss the chickens for roasting, following the method used in the Chef's techniques on page 62. Reserve the remaining herb butter to serve with the chicken as an accompanying sauce.

3 Heat a roasting pan on the stove top over medium-low heat. Add the oil and place the chickens on their side in the pan. Once the oil is hot, place the roasting pan in the oven and roast the chickens for about 10 minutes, basting with the pan juices every 5 minutes. Turn the chickens onto their other side and roast for 10 minutes, basting every 5 minutes. Turn the chickens onto their backs, add the chicken wings and roast for about 10 minutes, or until the chicken juices run clear, basting every 5 minutes.

4 Transfer the chicken and wings to an ovenproof plate, cover with foil and keep warm in a 250°F oven. Put the roasting pan on the stove top over low heat to clarify the fat, if necessary. After 5–10 minutes, without stirring, the fat should be clear. Pour off the excess fat. Strain the chicken wings of excess fat and return to the roasting pan. Add the vegetables and cook for 2 minutes, then add 2 cups water. Stir to loosen the cooking juices from the roasting pan, then pour into a saucepan. Bring to a boil, reduce the heat to simmer, skimming off the fat. Simmer for 35 minutes, or until reduced by three quarters. Strain into a smaller saucepan, discarding the chicken wings and vegetables. Whisk in the remaining herb butter, season and pour into a gravy boat. Remove the string and cut the chickens in half. Serve with the sauce poured over.

Smoked chicken and sun-dried tomato paté with black olive and caper relish

Patés baked in terrines are an impressive and elegant way to dress your dinner or buffet table, but a few slices served with a salad would also make an ideal first course or lunch.

Preparation time 1 hour 20 minutes + overnight
  refrigeration if possible
Total cooking time 1 hour 30 minutes
Serves 12

1 smoked chicken, about 2 lb.
4 large chicken drumsticks
2 egg whites
1 1/4 cups heavy cream
2/3 cup thinly sliced sun-dried tomatoes
1 1/2 cups chopped mixed fresh herbs

BLACK OLIVE AND CAPER RELISH
3/4 cup sliced pitted black olives
1/2 cup capers, coarsely chopped
1 clove garlic, chopped
2/3 cup chopped fresh chives
1 tablespoon olive oil

1 With a sharp knife, cut down each side of the breastbone of the smoked chicken, remove the wings and set aside the two breast pieces. Remove the skin and cut away the leg meat from the chicken, discarding the bones. Grind or finely chop the leg meat in a food processor and set aside.

2 With a small sharp knife, scrape the flesh from the raw drumsticks, following the method in the Chef's techniques on page 63. Trim away the fine, shiny, white nerves and tendons—these will not break down during cooking and will spoil the smooth texture of the paté.

Work the raw meat to a fine purée in the food processor, then blend in the egg whites. Transfer to a bowl, cover and refrigerate for 15 minutes.

3 Preheat the oven to 325°F. Sit the bowl of puréed chicken over ice and slowly mix in the cream to just blend. Season with salt and pepper. Gently mix in the smoked leg meat, sun-dried tomatoes and herbs.

4 Line the length of the base of a 6-cup terrine with a strip of doubled waxed paper or foil, to overhang the sides and help you unmold the paté after cooking. Half-fill the terrine with the chicken mixture, place the smoked chicken breasts on top and cover with the remaining chicken mixture. Cover the terrine with foil, firmly turning under to seal the edges.

5 Place the terrine in a baking dish and create a water bath by pouring in hot water to come halfway up the outside of the terrine. Bake in the oven for 1 1/2 hours, or until the juices run clear when tested with a skewer. Remove from the water bath and leave to cool in the terrine. The paté is best left refrigerated overnight to make slicing easier.

6 To make the relish, mix the olives with the capers, garlic and chives, then stir in the olive oil to bind. Loosen the edges of the paté with a sharp knife, then turn out and cut into 12 slices. Serve with the relish alongside.

Chef's tip In step 3, it is very important that the cream and meat purée be chilled. If not, there is a risk of the cream separating. If the cream separates, the smooth light texture of the paté is spoiled.

Chicken pie

Serve this delicious pie with simple boiled or mashed potatoes to mop up the chicken juices.
Brussels sprouts or spinach would also be delicious accompaniments.
Alternatively, for a crisper bite, serve with a mixed green side salad.

Preparation time **45 minutes + 30 minutes resting**
Total cooking time **1 hour 35 minutes**
Serves 4–6

I chicken, about 3 lb.
8 slices pancetta, about 6 oz., rind removed
1/4 cup unsalted butter
I hard-cooked egg, coarsely chopped
12 button mushrooms, quartered
I onion, finely chopped
1/4 cup white wine
I cup chicken stock (see page 62)
I sheet frozen puff pastry, thawed (see Chef's tips)
I egg, beaten
good pinch of chopped fresh herbs, such as parsley,
   tarragon or chervil

1 Cut the chicken into eight pieces, following the method in the Chef's techniques on page 63, and remove the bones and skin. Season with salt and pepper, then wrap each piece of chicken in a slice of pancetta and secure with cocktail picks or string.

2 Heat half the butter in a skillet over medium heat and lightly brown the chicken in batches, turning regularly to seal on all sides. Remove the chicken from the pan and drain on crumpled paper towels. Discard the cocktail picks or string and place the chicken in a 6-cup pie dish with the hard-cooked egg. Pour off the excess fat from the pan, add the remaining butter and cook the mushrooms and onion over low heat for 5 minutes without coloring.

3 Add the white wine to the pan and simmer until only a little liquid is left. Pour over the chicken. Add sufficient stock to almost cover the chicken pieces.

4 Roll out the pastry so that it is a little bigger than the top of the pie plate. Brush the rim of the plate with beaten egg and line with 1/2 inch of spare pastry cut from around the pastry edge, pressing onto the dish firmly and brushing with beaten egg. Fold the pastry over a rolling pin and cover the pie plate. Be careful not to stretch the pastry or it will shrink out of shape while baking. Press the edges together to seal. With a small sharp knife, trim off the excess pastry. Do not angle the knife in towards the dish or it will encourage shrinkage later. With the back of the knife, notch the cut pastry edge. Brush the top surface with egg, but not the edges. Make a small hole for steam to escape, then decorate with pastry trimmings and brush them with egg.

5 Chill the pie for 30 minutes, to prevent it shrinking during baking, and preheat the oven to 375°F. Bake the pie for 20 minutes, or until the pastry is risen and golden. Reduce the oven to 250°F and cover the pie with foil to prevent overbrowning while cooking the chicken through. Cook for 45 minutes. Break the crust in the center, or loosen and lift off from the side, and add the chopped fresh herbs. Serve immediately.

Chef's tips This pie has a lot of thin gravy; if you prefer a thicker sauce, roll the chicken pieces in seasoned flour after sealing and before putting in the pie plate.

Pre-rolled frozen puff pastry can be purchased in 171/4 oz. packages, each containing two sheets, from gourmet or specialty food stores.

Chicken liver salad with bacon and croutons

Chicken liver has a delicate flavor and soft moist texture when cooked. When pan-fried it is best served slightly pink in the center. Here, the sherry vinegar dressing cuts its richness.

Preparation time **15 minutes**
Total cooking time **15 minutes**
Serves 4

6–8 cups mixed salad leaves
6 oz. slab bacon, rind removed,
 cut into thin strips
1/3 cup oil
2 slices bread, crusts removed,
 cut into small cubes
14 oz. chicken livers
2 tablespoons unsalted butter
3 shallots, finely chopped
2 1/2 tablespoons vinegar

VINAIGRETTE DRESSING
2 tablespoons Dijon mustard
1/4 cup sherry vinegar
1/3 cup oil

1 Wash and dry the salad leaves and then refrigerate, covered with a clean dish towel, to prevent wilting.

2 Fry the bacon in a dry skillet over medium heat. Lift out and drain on crumpled paper towels. Set aside.

3 Heat the oil in a shallow skillet, add the bread cubes and fry, stirring, until golden brown. Lift out and drain on crumpled paper towels. Sprinkle lightly with salt and keep warm.

4 Clean the chicken livers, removing the small green area that can be bitter, and cut into small pieces. Heat the butter in a skillet and toss the liver over high heat for 2 minutes. Add the shallots and fry for another 2 minutes, then season with salt and pepper and transfer to a plate. The liver should be barely pink and juicy inside. Add the vinegar to the pan and heat to dissolve any of the sticky juices. Pour the juice over the liver and keep warm.

5 To make the vinaigrette dressing, put the mustard, sherry vinegar and salt and pepper to taste in a bowl and add the oil in a slow, steady stream, mixing continuously with a fork or small whisk until fully blended.

6 Put the salad leaves in a bowl, pour over the dressing and carefully toss to coat thoroughly without bruising the leaves. Serve topped with the bacon, croutons and liver with its juices.

Thai chicken wings

These crisp-skinned wings have the intense Thai flavors of ginger, cilantro and fish sauce.

Preparation time **15 minutes + 1 day marinating**
Total cooking time **1 hour**
Serves 4

12 chicken wings
4 cloves garlic, coarsely chopped
4 black peppercorns
1/4 cup chopped cilantro stalks or root
4 teaspoons finely grated fresh ginger root
2 tablespoons fish sauce (nam pla)
1/4 cup soy sauce
1/4 cup honey
2 1/2 tablespoons coarsely chopped cilantro leaves
2 scallions, cut lengthwise into thin strips

1 Wash the chicken wings and pat dry. Tuck the tip of each wing under the thickest part to make a triangular shape. Place in a nonreactive bowl and set aside.

2 To make the marinade, use a pestle and mortar to pound the garlic, peppercorns, cilantro stalks and ginger root into a paste. Add the fish sauce, soy sauce and honey and stir to combine. Pour the marinade over the chicken wings and turn to coat. Cover the bowl with plastic wrap and leave in the refrigerator to marinate for 24 hours.

3 Preheat the oven to 425°F. Arrange the chicken wings in a roasting pan in a well-spaced single layer and pour over the marinade. Bake for 1 hour, basting frequently, until tender.

4 Arrange the hot wings on a serving dish and garnish with the cilantro and scallions. You may wish to serve a dipping sauce such as chile sauce. Provide finger bowls and napkins as these are eaten with the fingers.

Stuffed chicken with celery root purée

A perfect combination of delicate and robust flavors with a syrupy mango chutney sauce—the finished dish is even greater than the sum of its delicious parts.

Preparation time **40 minutes**

Total cooking time **1 hour**

Serves 4

STUFFING

2 chicken thighs

1/2 cup plain yogurt

2–3 tablespoons chopped celery

10 oz. celery root, peeled and chopped (about 2 cups)

few drops of lemon juice

1/4 cup plain yogurt

4 skinless, boneless chicken breast halves,
    about 4 oz. each

1 tablespoon oil

1 tablespoon mango chutney

2 tablespoons sherry vinegar

2 cups chicken stock (see page 62)

1 tablespoon unsalted butter

2 tablespoons each of diced carrot, onion,
    celery and apple

1 To make the stuffing, remove the skin from the thighs and scrape the meat from the bones, reserving the bones. Weigh 6 oz. of the meat and work until smooth in a food processor. Add the yogurt, process until combined and transfer to a bowl. Add the celery and season wiht salt and pepper. Mix and set aside.

2 Add the celery root and lemon juice to a pan of boiling salted water and simmer for 20 minutes, or until the celery root is tender. Drain, return to the pan and shake over the heat for 1 minute. Purée in a food processor with the yogurt, season with salt and pepper and keep warm.

3 Preheat the oven to 375°F. Cut a slit in the side of each chicken breast, about two thirds of the way through, and spoon in the stuffing, avoiding overfilling. Heat the oil in a flameproof casserole or Dutch oven and lightly brown the chicken breasts. Add the thigh bones to the casserole and bake in the oven for 10 minutes. Remove the breasts, set aside and keep warm. Pour off the fat from the casserole, then add the chutney and vinegar and cook on the stove top until syrupy. Add the stock and cook for 10 minutes, or until reduced by a third. Season to taste, strain and set aside.

4 Melt the butter in a skillet, add the carrot, onion and celery and cook gently for 5 minutes, or until softened but not colored. Add the apple and cook for 2 minutes. Spoon the vegetables onto plates and top with the chicken breasts and sauce. Serve with the celery root purée alongside.

Chicken brochettes with vegetable rice

Brochette is a French word for skewer or kebab and is also the term for this method of cooking. Marinating the chicken before broiling on the skewers makes the meat more tender and flavorful.

*Preparation time **30 minutes + refrigeration***
   (1 hour or overnight)
*Total cooking time **1 hour***
Serves 4

4 skinless, boneless chicken breast halves
I large red sweet bell pepper, halved and seeded
12 button mushrooms
I onion
3/4 cup corn oil
1/3 cup soy sauce
juice of I lemon
2 tomatoes
I onion, chopped
1/3 cup white wine vinegar
2 cups chicken stock (see page 62)
I teaspoon chopped fresh thyme
2 tablespoons capers, rinsed and coarsely chopped

VEGETABLE RICE
oil, for cooking
I onion, thinly sliced
I cup long-grain rice
1/2 red sweet bell pepper, diced
1/2 green sweet bell pepper, diced
1/3 cup frozen baby peas, thawed

1   Cut each chicken breast into six cubes. Cut the red pepper into 12 rough squares. Remove and discard the mushroom stems. Halve and then cut the onion into large pieces to match the red pepper. Thread the chicken, red pepper, mushroom and onion alternately onto skewers and place in a shallow glass dish. Mix together the corn oil, soy sauce and lemon juice, spoon over the brochettes and baste well. Cover and refrigerate for at least 1 hour but preferably overnight.

2   To make the vegetable rice, preheat the oven to 400°F. In a flameproof casserole or Dutch oven, heat 2–3 tablespoons oil on the stove top, add the onion and cook gently until transparent but not colored. With a wooden spoon, stir in the rice and cook for 1 minute. Add 1 1/2 cups water and bring to a boil, stirring constantly. Season with salt and pepper. Cover the casserole and bake for 15 minutes, or until the rice is tender. Lightly mix in the red and green pepper and the peas and season to taste. Turn the oven to very low, cover the rice and return to the oven to keep warm.

3   Bring a saucepan of water to a boil and score a cross in the base of each tomato. Plunge the tomatoes into the boiling water for 10 seconds, then transfer to a bowl of cold water. Peel the skin away from the cross. Quarter and seed the tomatoes, remove the stems and coarsely dice the flesh.

4   Lift the brochettes from the marinade, reserving the liquid, and broil for 4 minutes on each side, or until the chicken juices run clear when pierced with a skewer. Transfer to a serving plate, cover and keep warm in the oven while you make the sauce.

5   Add the onion to the juices in the broiler pan and place over low to medium heat on the stove top, stirring until lightly colored. Add the vinegar and stir until reduced by half. Add the reserved marinade and cook for 2 minutes. Add the stock and cook for another 10–15 minutes, or until reduced to a syrup. Stir in the tomatoes, thyme and capers and season to taste. Serve with the sauce spooned over the top.

Chef's tip The brochettes may be prepared the day before and kept in the refrigerator overnight.

Chef's techniques

◆

Trussing for roasting

Rinse the bird inside and out, then dry with paper towels. Trussing the chicken helps it keep its shape.

Use ordinary household string to truss. Tie the legs together, wrapping the string under the tail first.

After the legs, take the string towards the neck of the bird, passing it down between the legs and the body.

Turn the bird over and cross the string over in the center, underneath the wings. Wrap the string around the wings to keep them flat.

Tie the string into a knot or bow to secure the chicken wings in place. Trim off the ends of the string and the chicken is ready for roasting.

Making chicken stock

Good, flavorsome homemade stock can be the cornerstone of a great dish.

Cut up 1 1/2 lb. chicken bones and carcass and put in a pan with a coarsely chopped onion, carrot and celery stalk. Add 6 peppercorns, a bouquet garni and 4 quarts cold water.

Bring to a boil and let the stock simmer gently for 2–3 hours, skimming off any scum that rises to the surface using a large spoon. Strain the stock through a sieve into a clean bowl, then allow to cool.

Chill the stock overnight, then lift off any fat. If you can't leave overnight, drag the surface of the hot strained stock with paper towels to lift off the fat. The stock can be refrigerated for 3 days. Makes 6–8 cups.

To freeze, boil the stock to reduce to 2 cups. Allow to cool and freeze until solid. Transfer to a plastic freezer bag and seal. To make 2 quarts stock, add 6 cups water to 2 cups concentrated stock.

Disjointing a chicken

The flavor of a dish will often be better if, rather than buying pieces, you cut up a whole bird.

Use a pair of poultry shears to cut through the length of the breastbone, then turn the chicken over and cut down either side of the backbone to completely remove it.

The backbone should come away in one piece. Then cut the bird into four pieces, following the natural shapes. You can also remove the wing tips at this stage, if you wish.

For eight pieces, cut each breast in half, so one piece has the wing attached, and cut through the leg joint to separate the drumstick from the thigh.

Bouquet garni

Add the flavor and aroma of herbs to your dish with a freshly made bouquet garni.

Wrap the green part of a leek loosely around a bay leaf, a sprig of thyme, some celery leaves and a few stalks of parsley, then tie with string. Leave a long tail to the string for easy removal.

Removing the wishbone

The wishbone is found at the neck of the bird. Its removal makes carving the breast easier.

Pull back the skin from the neck cavity. Use your fingers to feel for the wishbone just inside—you may need to slit the skin a little. Cut around the wishbone with a sharp knife, then scrape the meat away.

Cut away the wishbone at the joint and lift it out.

Scraping a drumstick

The darker meat on the chicken leg has a lot of flavor and is good for pâtés and stuffings.

Removing the meat from the bone can be fiddly. Pull the skin off the legs, from the fat end of the drumstick.

Hold the knuckle end of the drumstick and use a sharp knife to cut around the bone, then scrape away the flesh.

First published in the United States in 1998 by Periplus Editions (HK) Ltd., with editorial offices at
153 Milk Street, Boston, Massachusetts 02109.

Murdoch Books and Le Cordon Bleu thank the 32 masterchefs of all the Le Cordon Bleu Schools, whose knowledge and
expertise have made this book possible, especially: Chef Cliche (MOF), Chef Terrien, Chef Boucheret, Chef Duchêne (MOF),
Chef Guillut, Chef Steneck, Paris; Chef Males, Chef Walsh, Chef Hardy, London; Chef Chantefort, Chef Bertin, Chef Jambert,
Chef Honda, Tokyo; Chef Salembien, Chef Boutin, Chef Harris, Sydney; Chef Lawes, Adelaide; Chef Guiet, Chef Denis, Ottawa.
Of the many people who helped the Chefs test each recipe, a special mention to David Welch and Allen Wertheim.
A very special acknowledgment to Directors Susan Eckstein, Great Britain, and Kathy Shaw, Paris, who have been responsible for
the coordination of the Le Cordon Bleu team throughout this series.

The Publisher and Le Cordon Bleu also wish to thank Carole Sweetnam for her help with this series.

First published in Australia in 1998 by Murdoch Books®

Managing Editor: Kay Halsey
Series Concept, Design and Art Direction: Juliet Cohen
Editor: Jane Price
Food Director: Jody Vassallo
Food Editors: Dimitra Stais, Tracy Rutherford
US Editor: Linda Venturoni Wilson
Designer: Annette Fitzgerald
Photographers: Jon Bader, Joe Filshie, Chris Jones
Food Stylists: Amanda Cooper, Carolyn Fienberg, Mary Harris
Food Preparation: Michelle Earl, Jo Forrest, Kerrie Ray
Chef's Techniques Photographer: Reg Morrison
Home Economist: Michelle Lawton

©Design and photography Murdoch Books® 1998
©Text Le Cordon Bleu 1998. The moral right of Le Cordon Bleu has been asserted with respect to this publication.

All rights reserved. No part of this publication may be reproduced or utilized in any form or by any means,
electronic or mechanical, including photocopying, recording, or by any information storage and retrieval system,
without prior written permission from Periplus Editions

Library of Congress catalog card number: 98-65443
ISBN 962-593-435-9

Front cover: Chicken en croûte

Distributed in the United States by
Charles E. Tuttle Co., Inc.
RR1 Box 231-5
North Clarendon, VT 05759
Tel: (802) 773-8930
Fax: (802) 773-6993

Printed in Singapore

05 04 03 02 01 00 99 98 10 9 8 7 6 5 4 3 2 1

Important: Some of the recipes in this book may include raw eggs, which can cause salmonella poisoning.
Those who might be at risk from this (the elderly, pregnant women, young children and those suffering
from immune deficiency diseases) should check with their physicians before eating raw eggs.